Love Me Do

LYDIA MACPHERSON grew up in the sixties in a small village on top of the Yorkshire Pennines. She now lives in very flat East Anglia. Lydia has an MA in Creative Writing from Royal Holloway University of London. She has been placed in several competitions, including the Edwin Morgan Poetry Prize. Her poems range from the 'domestic gone awry' to the homeliness of the International Space Station.

Love Me Do

by

LYDIA MACPHERSON

SALT

CROMER

PUBLISHED BY SALT PUBLISHING
12 Norwich Road, Cromer, Norfolk NR27 0AX
All rights reserved

Salt Publishing 2014

Printed in the UK by Berforts Information Press Ltd.

Typeset in Paperback 9 / 13

ISBN 978 1 907773 69 3 hardback

1 3 5 7 9 8 6 4 2

For Robert and Sheila Sunderland,
for Felix and Hector Macpherson,
and for Nick MacKinnon

Contents

Acknowledgements

Some of these poems have appeared in *The North*, *Poetry London*, *Magma*, *The Rialto*, *Poetry Wales*, *Smith's Knoll*, *Seam*, *Iota*, *The Warwick Review*, *Days of Roses* anthologies, *Bedford Square 3* and the Templar Pamphlet anthologies.

Thanks are due to Andrew Motion, Jo Shapcott, Ann and Peter Sansom, Malene Engelund and Declan Ryan.

Antenatal

Sometimes when your fingers stray
into my mouth it hits me, a sudden
memory of swimming in the saline
Martian dark. Maybe eight months gone,
I float in Rothko roundness, rub up
along her copper-seven, against all odds,
an accident. I'm comfortable there
with my fists bumping my gums;
there's nicotine and alcohol
in psychedelic bands, subtly
altering cell structures, the flicker
of synapses.
          Maybe this is heaven
then, before it all got complicated;
wet and warm and neither longed for
nor rejected, with John and Paul
in another room singing *Love Me Do*.

Space Station

Alerted by the newspapers, we lean
against the barn's long wall to watch it track
the winter sky. It's hard to determine
the coordinates and maybe we'll mistake
it for a plane or star – but then, it's here,
sudden above the rows of sugar beet,
ploughing the night. We stand, in hugging awe,
heaven-struck like cavemen sighting a comet.

Rooted there, we cannot see the rickety
array of mirror tiles, the iridescent
bronzed haphazard symmetry,
outstretched like an emerging insect,
orbiting the earth-lit detritus of space,
bearing its cargo's gawky, weightless grace.

Ossuary

And when his father left
he learned to carve, to whet the blade,
worn arched and thin by years
of Sunday lunch, against the steel,
the Bakelite handle gentled
as a bird cupped in his hand.
Then, to test it on his thumb pad,
drawing the finest wire of blood.

Like marking former Soviet states
on maps, he portioned up a steer
in doodles on the fly leaves of
Philip's *Modern School Atlas*.
On the way home, his dinner money
bought a whole ox-tail, a fleshy
jointed dinosaur dripping its trail
through his satchel's hide.

It took a year of careful choice,
getting the right cut, saving
shoulder blades, ribs, hocks,
wishbones standing in for all
the delicate bits too hard
to find. The skull was worst,
a patchwork of chicken backs
and Christmas turkey leavings.

His father always said,
*'if a job's worth doing it's worth
doing well'*, and Dad would be proud,
he thought, to look under the single
bed and find, among the dust,
the furry sweets and Lego,
the bony keepsake, complete,
laid out upon the shagpile.

Europa

Ferdie, in the bar of the Europa Hotel.
You in your work boots and Murphys' fleece,
me just in from Aldergrove off a Hercules
full of the Hereford boys. Green,
heart banging so loud I thought
the dodgy trio at the juke box
would hear it. Guinness, of course,
which took an age to pour,
the barmaid signing a shamrock in the froth.
A double Jameson's for old times' sake.
The Europa, still standing, its windows wired with mesh,
and you, fresh from a meet by Lough Neagh
with the bad guys, still trusting me
to keep you safe and not yet waking to find
your father kneecapped and your boy dead.

Voodoo Barbie

You're Mattel play scale, one-sixth size,
made for fun in bubblegum pink plastic.
The painted lashes frame blue eyes,
your mouth an eager 'O' of coral lipstick.

Those nipple-less hard breasts mould
above the waist I had before the kids,
a coy gesture of hips which hold
no hint of messy sex or blood.

The smooth unbending legs taper
to crimped toes and cantilevered feet.
I'm hacking off your polyester hair,
skewering you with knitting needles,

decapitating your air-head fatuity,
dismembering you limb by perfect limb,
slitting that weird torso's cavity
to find no careful heart or womb.

You could have been a Barbie Doctor,
an Astronaut or Flight Attendant.
But you chose Barbie Family Wrecker:
I wish you barren disenchantment.

Curtains from Berlin

When his troops got to Berlin the first thing he did
was take down the curtains in Hitler's drawing room
and send them back to his wife in Epsom.
Unwrapping the brown papered parcel
she could smell foreign cigarettes and petrol
and as she shook out the crumpled silk
it was as if every flower had bloomed at once.

Such curtains! Lined and interlined, their hems
stitched with lead to keep them straight.
They made her want to tear down the blackout
and put the treasure on display like jewels
out of a long-locked safe. But, ever practical,
she took her sharpest scissors to them
and made dresses for her daughters
with neat bodices and full skirts,
for them to dance in on VE day.

The Cardigan

It was at the back of the airing cupboard,
pushed behind odd socks and a brown
hot water bottle. I think you
must have hidden it there so that
when I came back I wouldn't be upset.
The tissue paper, greying slightly,
cracked open to reveal
this egg-yolk woollen cardigan.
Not pink or blue, you see, but yellow,
to suit either a boy or girl, though
as you said, there were no girls
on your side for generations.
All that summer I had laboured
with the awkward casting on and off
of stitches: this tricky collar
alone had taken weeks. The tiny
cuffs are still rounded, waiting
for those fat wrists, my little chick,
blond of course like his brothers,
maybe a Hamish. There is a whisper
of talcum powder in this fine, soft wool,
and I can see myself sewing on
these six mother of pearl buttons
in a rush, before the icy trip
from Hoyle Syke to the hospital.
The row of ducks, so clumsily
embroidered, still swim
around the moss-stitch hem.

My Life and Times as a Bird

I wished I'd learned the language of the birds.
On the moor behind the farm I could not tell
the grouse were shouting out 'Go back! go back!'
so I played deaf and went straight in
to fifty years of silence. I should have known
the blue tit at the kitchen window
was tapping 'save yourself' in Morse.
Pacing through the broken rooms, from stone-flagged
hall to peeling parlour I heard a collared dove's
'It's pointless' from a twisted bully tree.
The books were slipping sideways, their losses
made to nests lined with Keats and R D Laing.

I stayed. Magpies brought me jewels:
sweet wrappers dropped by ramblers. The days
became too long, the house doll-small
under the rangy sky and in the bracken-hot
afternoons the robins sang of who killed who
and lapwings stood as witnesses in cotton grass.
I lived as almost owl, with blunted senses,
straining the dark for a mouse's footfall.
The meadow pipits were my alms-givers,
they pitied me with beetles and bilberries
smoked with the bloom of heather-dust.
I waited with a harrier's patience.

I knew I could not thrive as a bird.
The back end of the year went south.
The house fell under snow. I'd made my bed
of fallen feathers and sheep's wool barbed wire
leavings. I hollowed it by turning
round and round – the plover's trick – and slept
with my arms cupped over my head
like the wings of a broody hen on eggs.
The preying birds found their way in:
a merlin held my eye with hers. Outside
a muster of crows waited for my body's
dereliction. I was gone before the thaw.

Lessons

My darling, teach me how to love this bruise,
a swelling plum beneath my tautened skin.
The night's new fruit has grown in hours, contused
with rainbows. Show me, love, the beauty in
this loosened tooth, the rusty tang of blood,
its snag against my ripening lip – explain
the pleasure of this kick's adrenal flood,
the glory of the slap, the ministry of pain.
And curse me, sweetheart, spit, and educate
me in the ways of love with fists and fights,
the well-timed punch, the tender, delicate
last Glasgow kiss as you turn out my lights.
And, dear, by these lessons let me understand
this love, dealt by your soft, abusing hand.

Her Lovers

Before we take this further,
there are three things you should know.

First: at your left shoulder
are my five lovers.

Dave is slapping his palm
with a baseball bat.

Günter has the eyes
of my younger daughter.

Blond Benedict
cannot speak above a whisper.

There is poor Nicholas:
sad how thin he got.

And lastly Roberto,
tugging at his shroud.

Second: my mother has webbed toes
and a single figure handicap.

Third: well, we already know
about all that.

I am innocent in law.
Come. Kiss me, darling.

Miss Guest

in whiskery tweeds, upright, patrolling
the aisles of our desks where we sat
in obedient rows parsing Latin.
On the long cork board at the back of the room,
her pin-ups: Pliny, Xenophon and Cicero.
Gorgeous with hormones, we sneered at her,
a gently reared spinster who, we thought,
never knew the true meaning of *amo amas*.
But one day she read us Catullus
and the sun rose in the pale moon of her cheek.

Virus

A third floor room, the isolation
ward where slanted blinds
leak pearled aquarium light.
Green linoleum, the sedative hum
of nurses' voices along the corridor,
the honeycomb Braille of cotton blankets.
Permitted boredom in the filtered air,
no flowers, no visitors, just the coming
and going of temperature taking,
the careful handling of the thread
of mercury against my teeth,
my pulse bulging eagerly against
a capable finger, the charts to map
a journey of abandonment.
Pills in tiny plastic cups washed down
with stale-ish cordial from ribbed jugs,
baths taken Cleopatra-style with
milky water and the dangling
promise of a red emergency cord
should things get out of hand.
A voluntary submission to the rule
of tea at 6 a.m., Horlicks at dusk
and trays of school food to mark
the time passed in between.

The Petri dishes bloom in basement labs.
I want them to become a jungle of viruses,
I want to be tended here forever.

Armadillos

After landfall and prayers of thanks
the gold-seekers push through

the steaming forest, sweating
beneath their beaten metal,

chafed by the woven iron
which rusts and rubs.

At twilight they make camp
in a clearing among the cocoa trees.

The air is spiced with vanilla
and stirred by moths flowing

like orchid petals among
the buttressed roots.

One by one, they unfasten
their clanking skins, lay bare

the soft larval whiteness beneath,
protected by a crucifix or a tattoo:

the tender shoulders a canvas
for blurred hearts, anchors, scrolls

of curling indigo, protested love
of women, or faith in their God,

who, it seems, is not present here,
with the light fading

and the sad nocturnal
grunts and rustlings

of the armadillos,
those little armoured ones.

Love Letters

The oak desk in the college library
that dealt in English Lit and Norse
for me, then shape-shifted
for your Further Maths.
We traced our courtship on its grain,
quietly, with scratched diphthongs
and equations. I knew when you
had been there by the love letters
left behind in log tables.
You got smudgy runes beside
the tarnished light switch.
At the end of our last summer
we upped and left it to its own devices.

'Leeds Pottery mug, 1780, inscribed "Nanny Hartley drinking green tea" – possibly the Nanny born into the Hartley family at Baildon, Yorkshire in 1750'

You'd scarcely credit the cost of this tea
grown on Lord Howard's estate in Assam,
brought by clipper to Liverpool, carted
to Bradford on the pack horse way by Pendle.
I am the eldest: Miss Ann Hartley,
though I've always been 'Nanny'.
The younger ones made good:
Grace to John Hey, farmer at Eldwick,
Hannah to Will Kirk, quarryman
at Ilkley. Grace had this mug made
at Leeds to mark the thirtieth year
of my birth. In profile, as I am here,
the disfigurements barely show.

How straight I sit in the good chair,
how tiny my waist, how fine my lace-edged
bonnet, how voluminous my dark silk!

19

The number nineteen bus is moving through
the late morning, swaying in traffic
along Knightsbridge. On the top deck
heat is magnified by long windows
and here is a young man, restless
against the thin velour of the front seat.
Sweat soaks the padded collar
of his winter coat and beside him
is a rucksack, and he is watching it
as if it were his child, his son.
Some birds are singing as the bus leans
around Sloane Square, making for the barracks
where the new soldiers are parading,
with rifles mustered on this hot July day.

A Scarf from Africa

It's a long way from the Kruger, this piece
you bought me in the museum shop.
To remind me, you said, of those African skies
and the chill of pre-dawn on the high *kop*,

drinking local coffee from a thermos,
keeping an eye on the Cape buffalo
who turned their broad, grave faces
to watch our binoculared khaki tableau.

In our local bookshop's Starbucks
with a skinny latte and a macchiato
we look at your choice of phrasebooks.
Beneath my fingers the undertow

of other colours below the evident blue,
humming scarlet, a roughened black
drum and speak their own thready tattoo,
that now there is no way to get it back.

Delicatessen

I'm in your feral kitchen eyeing up
the women's names and numbers spread across
the whiteboard nicked from school. The table top
is waxed with grease, each cupboard's full of useless
cartons of the out of date and BOGOF trash,
your plates don't stack: here's Seventies naff,
here's mine, here's one your wife forgot to smash,
the cutlery is mismatched transport caff . . .
I want to fill you up with deli treats,
to load your shelves with damson confiture
and special salt, I want to make you so fat
with my nutritiousness that all your
trembling hands can do is take that sodden
dishcloth and rub those names out, one by one.

The Quarry List

(The British Association for Shooting and Conservation Pocket Guide to Quarry Identification)

Tufted duck. Red deer. Wigeon.
White-fronted goose. Grey
squirrel. Common Snipe. Rook.
Rabbit. Coot. Woodpigeon.
Pink-footed goose. Jay.
Mountain hare. Muntjac.
Red-legged partridge. Collared
dove. Chinese Water deer.
Woodcock. Gadwall. Magpie.
Greylag goose. Curlew. Mallard.
Ptarmigan. Sika deer. Brown hare.
Grey partridge. Goldeneye.
Black grouse. Pintail. Shoveler.
Teal. Moorhen. Jack snipe.
Fallow deer. Pheasant. Crow.
Golden plover. Canada
goose. Pochard. Scaup.
Roe deer. Red grouse. Jackdaw.

God's Own County

The people there are careful
with the way they dress:
it's important not to lose
too many feathers from the wings
pleated beneath their clothes –
the farmers' tweed jackets,
the milkmaids' smocks.
Despite the toffee and striped rock
no one's teeth go rotten.
They're smiling radiantly,
waiting for the Rapture,
when the rest of us invade in caravans.

We'll buy a takeaway communion
of clotted cream and cider, breathe
the incense of deep lanes and hedgerows
and, when the weather smiles,
release nappyless cherubs on the beach
while altar boys hold buckets and spades
behind the wind breaks' rood screens,
or wait out the rain in the limbo of cafes.
We'll hope for sun-polished halos
and find our faith in rock pools.

Perhaps, if I've been good,
they'll let me go there: to the outer limits,
phrased with clouds, curly with sea shores
and held by soft winds
which I think are called zephyrs –

not the car my Dad had way back when,
but little pink-edged gusts
filled with ozone and that sign of salt
you get at the end of the day.

1962

My mother, forever Jackie Kennedy,
flicking her eyeliner with an expert hand,
dusting just the right amount of rouge.
Sitting in front of that curtained kidney
dressing table, in her satin Maidenform bra
and matching pale pink cami knickers.
I am two, helping her fasten her suspenders
onto her stockings, my fingers stumbling
on the rubber dimple which must somehow slide
the American Tan nylon into its metal harbour.
I am bathed and ready for bed in my barred cot
and she is a bird of paradise with the aviary door
open before her.

2CV

The Deux Chevaux called Celestine,
with her umbrella handle gear stick
on the dashboard, the sardine-can peel
of her rubberised roof, flying back
when I hit sixty on the A40 near Oxford.
Her maroon paint work strangely matte,
like shutters on Provençal windows,
her special muff of grey plastic, inserted
like a diaphragm over her grille in winter.

The boy who begged my parents
to buy me something sensible,
then broke himself in his Ferrari Dino
on a moorland road. The long summer
of visiting him, her hot seats of stripy cloth,
her steady drone as she ate up the miles, thirty there
and thirty back, my gap year fellow traveller,
out to Scotton, back to Oxenhope.

I think he knew me
when I fed him, thought of him in Celestine,
young, and laughing in the whole world.

Sunday Afternoon with Svankmeyer and Popa

for Helen Ivory

First, she rolls it to a ball.
He takes it, moulds it into something
sharp and dangerous but then
she cradles it and talks nicely.
In time, he learns to speak
its language, but she is bored
of it by then, and turns it out
into a cold place. It waits
and finds another she who
plays the game with the old him.
They love and eat each other up
so that all that is left of it
are a few crumbs, breathing softly
in the happy ever after here and now.

Pastoral

The wireless bleats
spring is here and look
the chewing gum is blooming
lichen on city pavements
in the river shopping trolleys
are mating at rusty angles
welding in the petrol spills
all the roadside hedges
are neon with the scrumple
of carrier bags nesting
among the burger boxes
chrysalis condoms hang
in the scrub of lay-bys
and my young fancy turns
to thoughts of how
you pierced the robin's egg
and blew that promise
                    clean
                            away

Olive Oil

A lamp on your bedside table,
and always a small bottle of olive oil.
The label, grease spotted,
from the chemist in those days,
when the Co-op sold flour from bins
and a man brought milk in a cart.
Then, I could sit safe on your lap
in the faded striped deckchair,
hold onto your ear and suck my thumb.

A table spoon of olive oil when you woke.
Once you let me taste it.
Poured it out, medicine, bitter
on my tongue – and filled my head
with memories of that long battle
in Italy, the unaccustomed heat,
the Yorkshire mill lads lip-reading
across the zip and ping of bullets
on white-washed monastery walls.

There was a summer day
we shared lunch – tomatoes, bread
and first pressed extra-virgin.
I held your medals in my palm
then turned from my son's pram
to push your wheelchair
with such a practised ease and knew
your olive oil had not protected you,
that I must be our own patent remedy.

Jack

The year I turned eighteen,
and in every Bradford pub,
played out over the fog of Silk Cut
and lager tops, his Geordie words:
I'm Jack. In the *Telegraph and Argus*,
blurry worn-out women's faces:
every day, it seemed, a different one.
And going home after a good night out,
my brother driving our shared red Ford,
the roadblocks, the policeman
coming to my side: *Are you alright, love?*
The stories reeling round from mouth
to mouth, how a hitchhiking girl
stepped into a woman's car to find,
along the journey, her eyes drawn
to the driver's hairy hands.
I'm Jack. You think I'm clever, and I am.
Then, just as I left to go south, intact,
they found him, living in the suburbs
with tidy Sonia, who must have watched
us bad girls everyday, smoking
behind the school squash court,
and wondered where her good man was.

Lithium Lovesong

My element, seamed in stone
and tethered now between helium
and beryllium, a foil balloon pulling
at your moorings, your supple almostness
fingers gravity, kissing air and blackening
with it. As hard to cut as moonlight,
you're pulling me like a tide away
from knife drawers and cliff edges,
safety-netting my amygdala.

Unmaddened and inhibited,
I pop your blisterpacks like bladderwrack,
put on your drugged armour like some new crustacean.
You are the lulling surf in my heartbeat,
the ozone in my metalled mouth,
the wavering in my fingertip: take me
to the smooth sea's bed and tie me down,
wrap me up tight and level me,
let me learn to live a flattened life.

Guantanamo

(or, a poem from lines by Matthew Sweeney)

For white he used toothpaste,
for red, blood – but only his own.
For paper, a Styrofoam cup, guarded
like a daughter and pressed flat
beneath his mattress. By Allah's grace
his fingernails remained to trace
the words onto the bumpy palimpsest.
He wrote of nightingales in Karakul,
of apricots curved like a woman's breast,
the stream in his father's orchard in Herat,
how cool the water felt when
it flowed down his open throat.

Till Dawn

They say it's harder for those left behind,
so why do you keep trying to get back?
These days I'm sleeping with the lights on,
expert in the phases of the moon,
the early morning train times, the taxonomy
of moths. Even with my eyes screwed shut,
I note the clock's red flick as if you'd passed
a hand across my face. The milky drinks
in the small hours of the kitchen,
lit by the fridge's cinema glow, the burbling
background of the World Service,
its RP reassurance giving way to patriotic
music, weather continents distant,
the far flung potential of the shipping forecast –
nothing drives you off. How many years was it
before the ground had settled back to make
a headstone worth its while? That rose
your mother threw must have joined
you long ago in a slow dance of rot and growth.
It seems just yesterday that staying up till dawn
was all we wanted. Be careful what you wish for.
The chink of milk bottles, the baby's cries,
a two-tone siren streets away, all mark
the daily absences of life.

Walking the Woods

There had been talk of new beginnings,
leaves turned over, putting things behind us.

But I was all for letting the season
have its way with the trees.

The invitation to take a turn in the woods
was, I suppose, unexpected,

but not unwelcome, once I got used
to the idea of firewalking

and the foliage was of course
quite stunning that year.

People were soon accustomed to us
and kept to the marked paths.

Perhaps we became part of the scenery
like traffic and low flying aircraft.

So the sudden whoosh and solar flare
must have gone unremarked,

except by radio-astronomers
and seismologists on overtime,

that day you lit the blue touch paper
and forgot to retire.

Paint

Glossing over the knots and slits
with the slap and dash
of a cheap brush, you leave
the sugar soap and masking tape
on the shop shelf and just
crack on with five litres of magnolia,
my custard-skinny rival.
Your full-moon manic phase
will keep you up all night
like one of those TV shows
where a blonde girl
makes a palace with some MDF
and scatter cushions.

By 4 a.m. you're done. The paint
is setting in a cooling lava flow.
You leave one thumbprint
on my sleeping cheek.

Ikebana

Here's a frame of arms and legs,
fuzzy with new growth and sap.
He's jack-of-the-green for one day only,
wrapped in copper beech and breathing
his almost-man's sweat, tall
and private as ikebana, how
the Japanese might show the future
in a single red chrysanthemum
flowering just above his heart.

1969

The oak leaves crackle underfoot
like breakfast cereal; the mill siren
tells lunchtime; a car groans up the hill.

We are a pack of brown jumpers,
each one a small girl holding
her lunch in a Tupperware box.

The bracken is full of adders waiting to kill us.
The trees are dressed with spiders.
We must be alert to every possibility.

We are tired. Last night our parents
woke us up. Some men have landed on the moon.
We think that maybe we can see them now,

in that pale cut-out in the summer sky.

Siren Song

Put on your hat and row across the water;
you promised you would come if I should call.
Push out your clinker boat along the slip
below the dunes and make no sound,
let only starlight pull a trace
along your journey's gentle wake.

If you should come before I wake,
row softly over the still water,
open my door and let your footsteps trace
their way up to the attic room, then call
my name and let it sound
like plainsong drifting from your lips.

Pull off your boots and slip
beside me as the day awakes
and stretches to the sound
of birdsong flashing on the water,
as the sunlight starts to call
the dark away without a trace.

If snow starts falling, every trace
of us might vanish in the slip
of ice and flakes and you could call
forever and not wake
a soul across the frozen water
where winter stifles every sound.

The nights are long here on the sound
and wiser men than you might race
to get home safe over the water,
but stay a while and it could slip
your mind that you may never wake
from this dream of a siren's call.

Some say it's fate and others call
it luck to leave me sleeping sound
and plough a homeward-steady wake,
knowing you have lived to trace
some dark angel's smiling lips
in the ripples of the water.

But listen for the beckoning sound of water
and one day you will wake and hear my call,
slip back and trace your footsteps gladly to my open door.

The Burning of the Pets

Today they start the burning of the pets.
The wind is in the right direction,
the sky is blue and flecked with larks
and fighter planes, the weather's set
and it's as good a day as any to burn pets.

There are economies of scale and pets
who die before the rest must wait in piles
like fur coats on a party bed until
the latecomers catch up, collarless
and stiffening, for the bonfire of the pets.

They come in unmarked vans and pets
who, living, would have bickered now sleep
easily together, the Dobermans and flopsy bunnies,
tabbies curled with mice and gerbils, paws and claws
and hooves and tails, a jumbled bestiary of pets.

There are no funerals for the pets:
the forklift hoicks them down the chute
like laundry in a hospital, a button's pressed,
a fat man settles with his *Daily Sport* and tea
to wait for the incineration of the pets.

Tomorrow they'll box up the pets
in plastic urns of varied size:
a lucky dip of bones and teeth,
which, parcelled out to owners,
will complete the burning of the pets.

Hefted Ewes

Winter grips early this year
and we must find our places
in hollows worn out
by mothers and grandmothers,
knitted with heather roots,
lined with their cast-offs.
Here we turn our flanks
to the Pennine northerlies
and shoulder sleet hanks.
Our bellies full of life, though,
quickening with kicking hooves.
We remember our own spring:
how the blood-warm milk
brought with it our belonging,
hefted us to the moor, its thin
blue clearness, the curlew's call
among the cotton grass,
the connection of it all.

The Fisherman

You see him whenever your train eases
into a town's edge, framed by the concrete
lip of the bridge and the canal's skewed bank.
He's there at the five-rise locks in Bingley,
through the dazed windows of the sleeper
at Narbonne, or by the Dnieper one July.
Maybe the water gives back tower blocks,
poplars, a dead mill or the slow pull
of terraced houses up the moor side:
it's all the same to him.

He's got his flask and sandwiches,
a box of maggots and a keep net,
a folding stool that's seen some times:
that monster pike who knew the score,
the reel tick-tocking with his heartbeat
until the bugger broke the line
on the serrated pedal of a drowned bike,
or the kiss of a carp's pout as it teased
away the bait till all it left was the barb,
sticking two fingers up as it was wound in.

There's nearly always buddleia and dog shit,
maybe some kids messing up his chances.
The tunnel sprays a silver painted language
he can't understand, though he knows
the slowing and the quickening echo
of that train you're sitting on well enough.

As you lose sight of him and greet your
reflection in the dulling glass he's calling
it another day, packing up his kit,
heading back to the unlit house.

Pencils

We are the pencils, we're packed together
in neat boxes, or escaping on desks.
We make you shave us, you're our servants.
We are the pencils, sweating behind ears,
padded with rubber, sucked, chewed.
We play our disappearing trick on you;
we are the nutritious, clever pencils.

The Winter Outing of the Woolhope Naturalists' Field Club, December 1870

The ladies of the party are helped over the stile
by whiskered botanists fond of a well turned ankle.
Miss Taylor draws a notebook from her beaded reticule
and writes 'The bunch of mistletoe was so large
that it could be exceedingly well seen from the lane.'

The Reverend Johnson climbs the ladder
'placed with thoughtful consideration' amid banter
from the men about Druids, golden sickles
and garlanded white yearling bulls.

The Reverend drops the felted sticky bundle
and 'small sprays of the heaven born plant
unpolluted by any touch of earth' are given out
to 'all the ladies present'. Miss Taylor holds
the wishbone sprig with its smeary fruit.
Her whalebone stays are biting, her chilblains
ache, her hem is iced with mud. She smiles
(Mama says she must always smile).
In the dwindling light the botanists are advancing.

Invicta

Cherries in the glazed green bowl,
a pile of skin-split red-yellow,
and with them the confection
of deceit, the little fishing fly.
Filaments of jay feathers,
hackle of dyed seal fur,
the hidden barb which hooked
and brought the fruiting
bead of blood, and taught
how you have been played
on a hard line, run upstream
through deep river troughs, an
almost freedom until that hook
tugs your lip and brings you back,
to the cherries in your kitchen.

Night Song

for Mark Doty

No curtains for this little harbour room;
our walls are lined with moonlight's silver-gilt.
We lie like treasure in the tombs of kings,
our breaths are misty hieroglyphs in air
and, love, we learn to leave this world tonight.
This is how memory is made. Carved, gilded,
put away for years, patinated, found,
If we lie still in this soft gleaming night,
these fraying sheets will be our bodies' shrouds,
this bedside chest must bear our votive gifts:
whisky, essence of Rose Absolute, books,
Die Zauberflöte to see us to our next world,
the candle blinking its unsteady Morse,
the surf's insistent chant,

'Go. Don't go. Go'.

Unterlinden

Lucas Cranach the Elder's 'Melancholy',
Unterlinden Museum, Colmar

'In the foreground a dark angel sits and smirks,
her black wings folded, wreathed halo slipped.
She pares a stick with vicious downward strokes.
The shavings mound beside a dog, who sleeps

with knowing eyes half open. A table,
a pewter bowl of fruit: plums, grapes and figs.
At middle distance, three putti gambol,
raise fattened goblin hands. A fourth swings

across a lowering landscape, right to left.
In the chiaroscuro background, trees
bend to an unseen divine breath
which brings this cloud of vanity, greed,

lust and death, epitomised in masquerades
of ribald men, riding boar and goat and ox ...'
Outside, under the lime trees, you shade
your eyes against the sun, order the Cokes.

Magpie Funeral

Dr Marc Bekoff, an animal behaviour expert, has claimed that magpies feel grief and even hold funeral-type gatherings for their fallen friends and lay grass 'wreaths' beside their bodies.

One for sorrow. No need to greet you,
Mr Magpie, hedgerow gangster,
fledgling-killer, thief. Iced,
an eye already gone, those alert angles
of pinions and tail feathers bent

with the drag of rain, that split
beak drooling blood. Laid out
among the last of the windfalls,
their cider sweetness masking your
sharper memento mori.

The mob of mourners flap down,
done up in streetwise monochrome,
machine-gun voices muffled,
the bling of tin foil and milk bottle tops
left in scrappy nests in beech trees.

In turn they hop forward, pause
a moment as if recalling you,
a fallen comrade, then place
a blade of grass on your corpse:
your winding sheet, your wreath.

In Jim Ede's House

Kettle's Yard, Cambridge

Your walls are twenty different shades of snow
as sound and light get filtered into stillness.
Eighty-three thin stones duet with their reflections
on the Bechstein's lid like shells spread out
on beaches at the end of a long day's rain.

And, though we know we cannot touch,
I'm holding out for your blessing
among the dip and swoop of bowls
and sculpture, a half-burned candle,
a vase more beautiful for being broken.

We're told the maker exits when the work is made,
but you remain, filling the spaces
and, among your other pieces, here I am,
arranged, curated, taken care of.

Nothing beyond it

Sometimes I wish I was still there, on the edge
of consciousness, with people sitting beside me,
asking my name. The hot crinkle of a foil blanket,
how beautiful it was to be held in the arms
of a blue-eyed man who told me everything
was going to be alright, how lovely to feel
the 'sharp scratch now' and then

                              the cosy slide
to somewhere orange and pulsing with pinpricks
of purple stars with creatures like jellyfish
circling and in the background Rostropovich
playing Bach's Cello Suites then

                              back again
to a narrow bed with metal rails and something
strange inside my throat and my mother
saying 'I'm sure she can hear me' and that
cello, singing over and over.

Glut

You should have followed
and kept me company
today among the hedges.

So many rosehips!
the obscenity of them,
taut and pert and waxed,

each seedpod ready
and straining. And
the blackberries –

how you would have loved
their stain, my mouth
stopped with them,

the spiked tangle
of my questions
silenced by their glut.

A Photograph of Ted

I came back from the fiesta in Alicante
to find this picture on the villa's oak bureau.
You are photographed on a rocky shoreline:
I hoped it was the Mediterranean, but it is not.
That coast behind you must, I think, be Devon.
Trousers rolled to just below the knee,
a workmanlike twill, dark blue perhaps.
A short-sleeved shirt, open at the neck,
maybe Aertex, or finely checked –
it's hard to tell from this many years away –
but it looks well-worn, a favourite of yours,
tucked in loosely. Unusually, you are smiling broadly –
I am used to those moody portraits. And yes,
I can see you are very young and very handsome.

The fishing line swings from your left hand,
and I had hoped the catch was fat sardines,
which you would take back, in the Spanish heat,
to the little honeymoon ground floor flat
and cook for lunch on the rudimentary stove,
before taking her to bed for a long siesta.
But now I see the fish is bait, a half mackerel.
You are about to cast it out, not bring it home.

Biology

The science lab is sick with Bunsens
as we file in to let Miss Platt
do battle with our ignorance.
We are the arty girls with hanks of messy hair,
hoping to crack biology as Miss P bastes
the Petri dishes one last time with agar-agar,
deals out pipes of bacilli for us to pinprick
out across the slime. She knows
she cannot alter us: the index in her head
reads 'locust', 'ox-eye', 'drosophilus'
and ours is 'Hardy', 'Homer', 'Isherwood',
the blue-eyed bad boy on the morning bus.

Afghanistan

Afghanistan lies behind a turquoise veil
which sometimes snags on mountain peaks
and turns into rivers, valleys and orchards.

There are nightingales everywhere,
who must sing to drown out those other
night fliers: not fireflies, or moths,

but those green and ragged creatures
which speak fire, and shake out men
attached to thistledown, who drift

like little gods into the villages,
handing out bullets like coins
to children at scarlet weddings.

Twelve Bore

You forgot it when you left. In your rush to go,
to shake me off the way a dog might dry itself –
instinctively, centrifugally – it was overlooked.
Lost in tweed and walking boots, it waited out
the heat of long days, missed a Glorious Twelfth.

How beautiful it is! The figured walnut stock,
made to fit your shoulder, moulds against me
like a husband. The scrolled engraving is worn
smooth here by the quick rub of first
your father's, then your ungloved fingertips.

The steel barrels are blued like starling wings
and smell of oil and gunpowder. They slip
beneath my novice hands like animals
or children. I'm steadied, lips parted,
eyes shut, breathless for your final kiss.

The White Peach

In the hothouse, Jos holds a rabbit paw
tied to the end of a bamboo cane.
The foot is shrivelled, the fur not worn
but heavy, somehow, with the strange
importance of its task. A smudgy wand,
it moves among the pink flowers,
brushing pollen between stamens and
naked stigmas which blush now
with the shy intimacy of gold dust.
Jos is an Edwardian, in cream flannels
and panama. Never married, and just
glad to have settled for this, the fertile
gilding of the white peach and, later,
the sound of honey bees in the border.

Surveillance

When it became unsafe to follow,
the GPS took over from us,
but the woods were listening to him:
the mushrooms like satellite dishes
tuned to the frequency of the dark,
the puffballs' geodesic domes
straining the beechmast static.

He had a wicker basket, a badger-hair
shaving brush and an Opinel knife,
an origami of rusty steel.
Back at the office reports were written:
routes taken, brief contacts,
phone calls made and received.

We didn't record how he lined his basket
with oak leaves, how he sang something
in his language and how he kissed his wife
on his return to the embassy.

There are days when I can see a car
with diplomatic plates and still
keep breathing. There are days
when I do not remember the way
his hair fell across his face.

Conjoined

When the evening show is over,
she cold creams off our greasepaint,
I unclip each pearly earring.

We brush our hair two hundred times,
to rid it of sawdust, sequins, the stench
of gunpowder and tigers.

The gentleman wants us *au naturel*,
but we still use our box of tricks –
essence of musk behind our ears,

talc veiling the startling furrow of our hips,
paste emeralds in our mirrored navels,
some rouge over four girlish nipples.

When he leaves us, spent and cursing,
we lie, sharing our breath like lovers,
the overworked arteries settling.

Big Bang Day

the Large Hadron Collider is activated

And then . . . and then the dwarf took up his pistol
and shot the rosary from the wall.
As the blind bride bit her tongue off
saxophones played violet chords.
Women ululated from the watchtowers
as barmen poured out bourbon
in the bodacious nymph's best glasses
and Elvis left the building (*you were
always on my mind*) and headed out to Vegas
in a bombproof sky blue Buick.
The protons and electrons were contemplating
close encounters with a billion soft murmurs
while six fishwives peeled the babies
and slowly sang them back to sleep.
I think you said you loved me
just before the stars exploded and the icicles caught fire
as the hordes of rakish parsons
raced beneath the chocolate mountains
to four white coated horsemen's tumultuous applause.

My Pink Artisan Kitchen Aid

pillowed in your quilted white cover,
sitting in state on the work surface.
How long I saved for you, like a bride
laying down her bottom drawer.
Your fleshy curves speak of an ability
to turn out sponge cakes at will,
your beater's unique planetary action
forces sugar to meet butter in a new
universe where moons of egg yolks
spin in its grip before succumbing
to your insistent charms. Your
accompanying recipe book throbs
with rum babas and meringues
and I am sorry, I've neglected you:
Now you will make me pay, now
is the time to master macaroons.

Chrysalis

I hadn't been back in years,
but you had waited,
the breathing machine pushing
life into you, your fingers
arranged on the white blanket
like smuggled ivory.
You were a chrysalis:
I wanted you to disappear,
to shed that ulcerated skin,
to see your lungs take flight
like butterflies and your heart
to flare once and then melt
with the rest of you
into the high summer air.

Nabokov's Butterfly Net

The hunting days are over. Migrated
to the old house in Petersburg,
it is pinned under museum glass.

The worn grip of perforated rubber
swells and yields in a black curve.
A pale steel rod spits its length:

a metre or so, long enough
to be demanding to handle.
Then, the articulated contraption

which joins the lip of the net,
almost a sleight of hand, the way
it tricks the hardness into its first

encounter with the open mouth.
The metal 'O' is slotted into
stiff canvas: once white

but stained now with pollen,
grass, the dust of a blue wing.
And then, the net: a crumpled

douche of tarlatan, that half
forgotten fabric which the
caption defines as a loose

weaved muslin once used
to make starched dresses
for ballerinas and debutantes.

Seals at Scolt Head

The dead live here: they lean against
each other in sleeky piles, stopping
the easterlies, never cold, just
gathered in companionable heaps.
They're wrapped up in their oiled
fur coats, whiskers radaring
for those who've lost their way,
out beyond the shipping lanes.

From time to time another leaves
or joins: it's casual, this death –
a green slip across the shoreline,
a welding of fingers,
the joining-up of feet, the new
elongation of the body.

They are unearthly now.
Water is their element, beyond
breath or gravity. Watch them
trailing cast-off bubbles
like snipped shrouds – they are
dancing for the straight joy of it,
the forgettingness.

After Vuillard

Sitting at your table, we are imprinted
with the sun, and oily with Ambre Solaire.
The green curtain blows in, carries exhaust fumes
from the overcrowded coast, stirred up
with narcotic lavender, with Gitanes
and rose-geranium. There are turquoises
at my throat: you bought them in Peshawar,
just after the snow-melt. Ice clinks
in thick, chipped, glasses and you perform
that alchemy with Pernod, the acid-green
turned milky-soft. Finger printed memory.
Strange how we only hear the swallows'
song as they prepare to leave.